LEARN TO

DRAW PENCIL

PORTRAITS

STEP-BY-STEP PENCIL DRAWING

TECHNIQUES AND SECRETS FOR

BEGINNERS AND INTERMEDIATES

– IN A FEW DAYS YOU WILL BE

DRAWING LIKE A PROFESSIONAL!

DANIEL STERN

IN THIS BOOK YOU WILL LEARN:

– How to think like an artist – why you are unique, and how and why you need to retrain your mind to unleash your potential to become a professional artist

– The best materials to use – Types of paper, pencils, erasers, blenders and so on.

– Drawing and Shading – Refining your lines; Breaking down nature into its basic fundamental shapes; How to depict tonal gradations in your art.

– Important landmarks of the face. Subtle differences between male and female, old and young, among different races.

– How to use a Proportional Sketch or Grid Sketch in your make-or-break initial layout.

– Important tips to ensure an accurate resemblance of your subject in your pencil portraits.

– How to create those extra touches to establish your style and ensure your portraits stand out!

TABLE OF CONTENTS

DEDICATED TO:

My Dad, who introduced me to the Wonderful World of Fine Art.

And My Son, who had already introduced himself to Art before I could!

INTRODUCTION

Hello! My name is Daniel Stern.

I've been handling a pencil for as long as I can remember...from watching my dad teach sketching and painting to his college students, to the still life drawing assignments he gave my brother and me every week (Thanks, Dad!)

Fast forward two decades later, and I'm still holding a pencil (and sometimes a paintbrush). I hope in the following pages to transfer some of my skills – and passion – for drawing I have kept over the years, from my dad as well as numerous other mentors and books I have absorbed since then.

Chapter 1. WHAT MAKES YOU AN ARTIST?

So you want to be an artist?

You want to be one of those people that goes around doodling on paper, or that brandishes paintbrushes looking for any surface even slightly resembling a canvas to paint on?

You have probably gotten used to the knowing glances, the expressions "I always felt he/she was a little eccentric. Now this explains it!" Or probably less frequently, "Ooh...but what a lovely picture. You are really quite talented!"

Of course, if you have been drawing or painting for any length of time (or just trying to learn) you would realize that the comments or views of people are not really what motivates you. But no, you are driven by the desire to improve your abilities, to become more skillful at reproducing the pictures you see in your head or in front of you...which is probably why you picked up this book.

Art is all about observation, you know. What makes you unique from 90% of the world (who are not so gifted) is your ability to note details that they would otherwise ignore. Normally, the supercomputers that are our brains work so fast at processing data that numerous tiny details at the fringe of our consciousness are either ignored or automatically processed while our minds speed on to their conclusions.

As a result, often when we begin our forays into art we carry a lot of preconceptions – how round a face is supposed to be, how high the eyebrows should be, how to depict the eyes, etc.

Many of these preconceptions are inaccurate, however. If they were not, everyone would be a terrific artist! This is why many professional artists advocate you use references for your subject matter. Once your eyes do not have a reference material to pick details from, your mind goes into default mode and relies on its preconceptions built from memory.

Whether as an artist you are going to be rendering portraits, still life compositions, landscapes/seascapes, or even comics and other illustrations, your skill will develop in proportion to your ability to isolate and identify those little details: the quirk of an eyebrow, a double wrinkle line or distinctive pair of crow's feet.

Your success will be measured by how faithfully you can reproduce your subject, and nowhere is this more painfully obvious however, than in portraiture. A wrongly placed eyebrow, improperly stretched eyeball, would be more than enough to make a completed portrait seem 'off'. And for many of us with our first few score (or first few hundred) portraits this is caused by those miniscule details that we subconsciously tell ourselves 'do not really matter much anyway'.

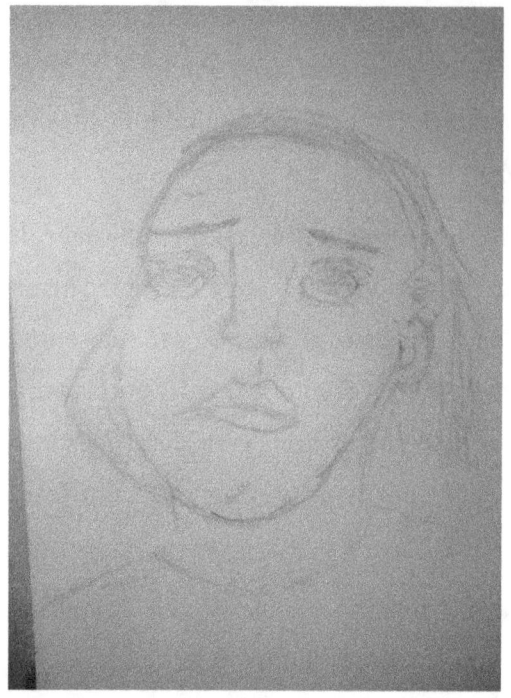

An example of a first portrait by my son David

However, worry not! These are steps on the path to greatness and professionalism that even the greatest artists had to take, so you are not alone. All you need to do is to keep honing your attention to detail – keep training and retraining your mind not to ignore those tiny facts – and keep assimilating and practicing the numerous techniques you learn along the way. Practice, practice!

Before you know it, people would be remarking at your pencil portraits "Wow. What a masterpiece. What great talent!" and you would probably say to yourself "If only they knew what it took to get here!

ACTION STEPS

Get a sketchbook (we'll tell you more about the best ones available in the next chapter). Get a photograph of your favorite relative or celebrity and do your best portrait sketch on one page. Don't worry how 'nice' it looks! This and several other sketches you'll make of the same photograph will help you monitor your progress as you acquire new skills during the course of this book.

CHAPTER 2. PAPERS AND PENCILS – BASIC INFORMATION YOU'RE BETTER OFF KNOWING

This section is all about the materials you're going to need to create that next great masterpiece. In order of importance, they are:

1. Paper

2. Pencils

3. Erasers

4. Ruler

5. Blending tool(s)

6. Grid paper

7. Stencils, etc.

1. PAPER

There are several things you need to know about paper - its size, weight and grain or texture. While some of this information may already be familiar, it is always good to get a refresher. And if you have not heard any of this before, then prepare to be enlightened!

SIZES

Paper comes in numerous sizes. The commonest is A4 which is usually used for printers, etc. Letter size is similar, though slightly longer. Letter size is 8.5 inches wide by 11 inches wide; A4 size is measured in millimeters (210mm by 297mm). An easy way to remember them is in the diagram below:

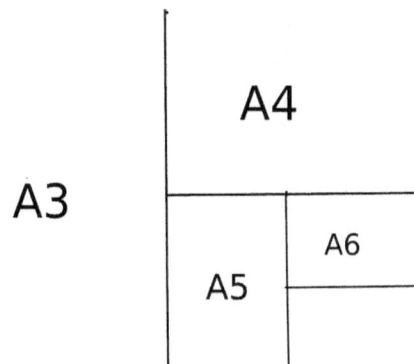

Different paper sizes, A3 – A6

Most computer programs like Adobe Photoshop or Illustrator can show you the dimensions of the paper you want to use. Just click Ctrl-O (Cmd-O in a MacBook) and looking at the different dimensions in millimeters or inches. Most sketchbooks come in the size A3.

PAPER WEIGHTS

This refers to the thickness and 'substance' of the paper. Quality artist's paper comes in different weights, from 120gsm, 200gsm (grams per square meter), up to 300gsm and rarely above. The weightier the paper the costlier, but the less likely it would be to be eroded or scratched away by erasers or other abuse, and the more resistant to bending or warping.

I would advise you use lighter paper, e.g. 120gsm for initial sketches, and heavier paper for portrait commissions and other serious work. In comparison, the common A4 printer's paper is only about 80gsm.

Please do yourself the big favor of investing in only quality artist materials from the start. Buy reputable names like Daler Rowney, Winsor and Newton, Derwent, Faber Castell, Staedtler, Royal and Langnickel and others. Most of these can be bought online from Amazon, or from any local art supplies store worth its salt.

GRAIN

This refers to the texture or 'tooth' of the paper. For rough sketches you probably wouldn't need a particularly smooth texture, but for tighter, more detailed artwork you would need paper with less texture.

'Cold-pressed' paper is suitable for most watercolor sketches and usually has a rougher grain and more tooth than 'hot-pressed' paper. A 'toothy' paper would be especially useful if you're painting with pastels and you need to render a multi-layered effect. But if you want to produce detailed, photorealistic pencil portraits or colored pencil paintings, 180-300gsm hot-pressed watercolor paper would be the way to go.

ACID-FREE OR NOT?

Lastly, you would want to ensure that the paper you use for serious work is as much 'acid-free' as possible. Acid-free paper has been processed such that it is less likely to react with the moisture and chemicals in the atmosphere, and thus it would be more durable and less likely to yellow with age.

2. PENCILS

We would be focusing strictly on lead (that is, graphite) pencils in this book, to avoid confusion. Other drawing alternatives and supplements like black and white charcoal pencils, charcoal sticks, Conte, and pastel pencils we'll leave until you are more confident with this medium.

What 'lead' pencils contain is not lead which is actually poisonous, but graphite. Graphite pencils cover a wide range, from the 6H, 5H, 4H down to H, F and HB, then the B's, 2B, 3B up to 9B. 'F' and 'H' pencils are hard and make lighter marks on paper; the higher the number the harder the graphite and the lighter the mark made, thus the harder you would need to press the pencil to make visible marks. 'B' pencils are soft and make darker marks on paper; the higher the B number, the softer and darker the graphite marks on paper.

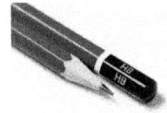

Diagram of graphite pencils

So the H pencils are useful for making light lines, and the B pencils are more suitable for shading. As you would imagine, 9B pencils would give you the softest and darkest shadows.

In actual practice you would only need three or four well-spaced pencils that would enable you reproduce all the necessary shades of light and dark. You may wish to purchase an H or HB pencil for your preliminary sketches, but a 2B could do just as well. Personally, with an HB, 2B and 6B I'm good to go.

ONE PENCIL TO 'LEAD' THEM ALL

Increasingly nowadays, more pencil artists prefer to use a mechanical pencil.

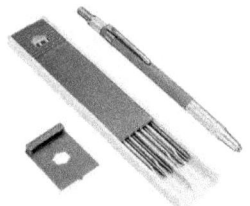

Mechanical pencils are more convenient to use because they do not require to be sharpened – you just replace the lead. This also makes them cheaper to purchase and maintain; a set of 12 or 24 refill leads can be got for very cheap. The disadvantage is that you have a narrower range of tonal values to exploit, but some people do very well with that, anyway – a mechanical pencil with a pack of 2B leads for example could still achieve a wide range of values. (We'll talk about tonal values in another chapter.)

3. ERASERS

You would need at least two types of erasers. The first is a large white soft eraser, such as that sold by Rotring. It would be much gentler on your paper than the common cheap erasers you find in most kindergarten classes. Under no account should you use any of those – when trying to erase soft pencil marks, they are more likely to smear the graphite deeper into your paper, thus making it all the harder to clear your mistakes.

The second type of eraser you need is a Kneaded or Putty Eraser. This softens and can be pulled apart and kneaded in the hands. It is invaluable for lifting off (as against rubbing out) graphite marks, and is especially useful when you need to lighten a dark area or bring out a highlight. You would apply it by dabbing it against the paper, not rubbing it as you would a regular eraser.

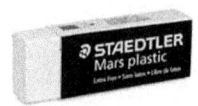
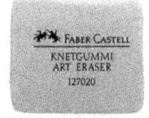

4. RULER

Like we said earlier, a ruler is good for...drawing straight lines, depicting perspective and making measurements. It is especially essential when delineating important landmarks of the face, whether you are using a grid or doing a freehand proportional sketch.

A transparent ruler is advisable, as it would enable you see your work underneath.

5. OTHER STUFF

Most other materials you could make for yourself, at least until you can afford more expensive stuff. These include:

SMOOTHING TOOLS

You could use cotton ear buds, or (I'll cringe to say it) your fingers for larger surfaces.

Definitely you'd have to have a handy tissue close by to wipe the oil from your fingertips – but more on that later.

Of course you could get a set of tortillions or blending stumps, if they are available and you can afford it.

ARTIST'S FIXATIVE

You would also need to protect your finished work, particularly if you are not framing it behind glass immediately. Even if you are, it would still be wise to invest in a quality fixative to prevent any smudging of your finished masterpiece.

PLASTIC STENCILS

These tools help increase the accuracy of the shapes you wish to draw. For example, you could have a stencil of different-sized circles, French curves, etc. They could also come in useful when you need to erase specific areas of your work while leaving the rest untouched.

CHAPTER 3. LINES AND SHAPES

The line is a fundamental element of nature, and of drawing. Every pencil artist begins with a line, for this is what lifts your subject out of, and differentiates it from the white paper around it. What distinguishes you as an accomplished draughtsman or a good pencil artist is your control of line and your ability to bend it to your slightest whim (yeah, I just had to say that).

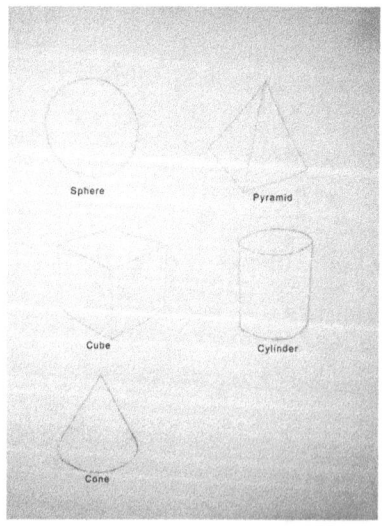

Some good watercolor and oil painters and even digital artists are not very good draughts-men. It's easy to cover up for this with paint, however when you have to do illustrations or you have only graphite as your medium, you just have to master it.

Fortunately, this is not as difficult as it sounds; it just takes practice. It also takes realizing that every form in nature can be broken down into five basic shapes, as seen in the diagram above.

Okay, let us back up a bit.

Remember I said that as an artist you would have to retrain your mind to notice details where most other people cannot? Well, we are beginning to put that into practice. And one of the first things you need to do is to think in 3D. One of the details automatically ignored by our minds when we draw our first pictures is that of depth. Hence the flat two-dimensional sketches we often draw. Depth (an illusion of three-dimensionality) is one of the first things we need to include in our drawings.

The five basic shapes may be less apparent in naturally-appearing forms in nature compared to man-made objects, but they are always there nevertheless.

Take the human head for example: the forehead is a modified hemispherical dome; the eyes are spheres set into the sockets of the skull; the nose is a half-pyramid with two hemispheres at the base.

In the next chapter we will see how learning to shade these shapes properly would enable us introduce more realism into our portraits.

ACTION STEPS

Practice drawing the basic shapes yourself in your sketchbook – the cube, sphere, pyramid, cylinder and cone. Begin to take a fresh look at nature around you, looking out for these shapes. They may be more difficult to detect in people and animals, but soon you would realize that everything is built up on these shapes, or modifications of them.

Chapter 4. Value and Shade

In the last chapter we talked about the five basic three-dimensional shapes found in nature. In this chapter we would look at one of the most important elements (among perspective and others) that is essential in enabling our eyes recognize the solidity or three-dimensionality of subjects.

That element is one of light and shade, or value. Look at the clean line drawing of a young lady below:

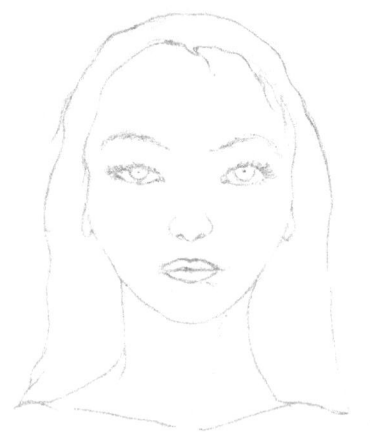

Now look at a drawing of the same woman below, shaded:

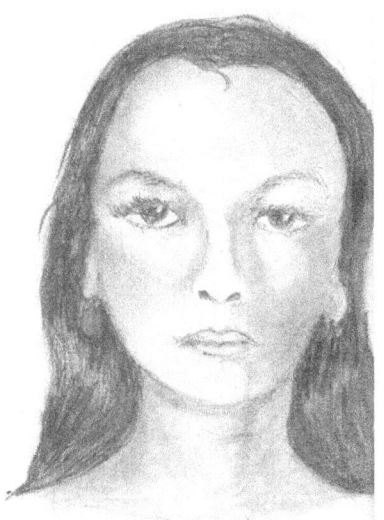

The difference is as night and day, isn't it? This is a graphic way of portraying the importance of value in our drawings. Shading is the only way we can show with graphite the differing values of color that we see otherwise in nature.

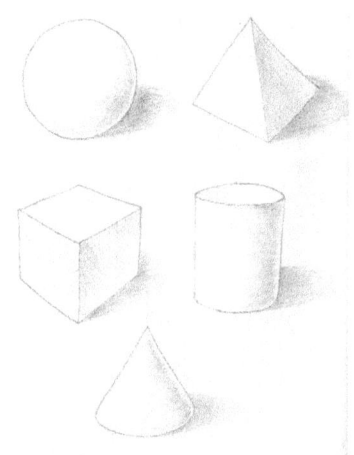

HOW TO SHADE

1. HATCHING – in this method we draw numerous fine lines in one direction, along the shape of the object. To achieve realistic effects, you would need to layer many strokes gently to build up value.

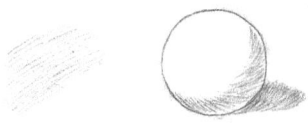

2. CROSS-HATCHING – similar to hatching, but in addition we draw many fine lines at ninety degrees to the initial strokes.

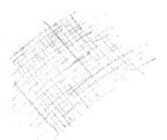 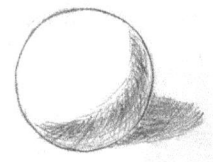

3. STIPPLING – this is the process of applying numerous dots and dashes to the areas we want to shade. This is sometimes useful for creating unique effects, e.g. pointillism-like effects, hair stubble, etc. To achieve darker areas, you would apply more dots/dashes.

This effect looks really nice sometimes, but could be rather tedious to execute.

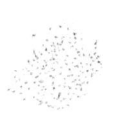 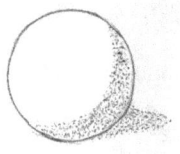

4. SCUMBLING – in this method we make gentle circular motions on the paper surface with our pencil, until the intended area is covered completely. This method makes it especially easy to go back in and blend the

shading, but the others except stippling can be equally blended.

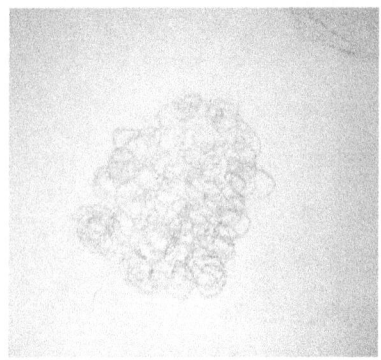

5. BLENDING – some graphite 'purists' disdain and thumb their noses at blending, preferring to keep their hatching or cross-hatching lines visible in the shading. My opinion is...to each his/her own.

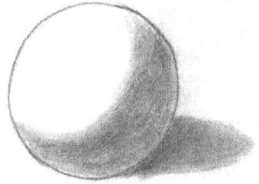

The beauty of art is, use whatever works for you and what you feel most comfortable with. Still, there are subtle variations in value that you may find it impossible to achieve, especially in your earlier works, without blending – unless you have hundreds of hours to spend on an individual art piece.

This is where the tortillions we mentioned in our shopping list earlier would come in useful. Tortillions (or other adapted instruments like cotton ear-buds for example) are useful for blending small areas, while you could use your fingertip (wiped dry of skin oils and sweat) to blend larger areas of graphite.

CREATE A TONAL GUIDE

The purpose of creating a tonal guide is to enable you compare values when shading. We are trying to represent the colors we see in nature with shades of graphite, so having a tool with which you can make quick comparisons would be quite useful.

All you need to do is to draw ten square blocks, each about an inch (about 2.5cm) square. Using a 2b pencil, shade in the squares lightly from the second to the tenth. (We'll be leaving the first square completely white.) As you proceed, shade each square a little darker until you get to the tenth, which would bear the darkest shade possible with your pencil. Presto! You now have a tool you can use to compare your photo subject's values to those in your drawing.

ACTION STEPS

Have you made a tonal scale like we just explained? If not...well, what are you waiting for?!

You could repeat the exercise once or twice on different strips of paper – you could only get better with practice. That way, you could pick your best attempt and discard the others.

CHAPTER 5. IMPORTANT FACIAL LANDMARKS

Though this is but an introductory overview that we would go into detail with later on, it is necessary we realize that there are certain anatomical similarities common to most people – despite the wide variety of facial features.

These are general principles we need to watch out for when rendering faces. A firm grasp of them ensures that our portraits appear more true to life.

AGE

An imaginary line passing through the eyes would also clip the tips of the ears. This line would separate the forehead and eyebrows from the other features 'down below'. In babies it divides the face into two halves. As one grows older however, this line moves upward...such that the features occupy a larger area and the forehead a smaller portion of the entire face. The hairline also recedes (in men at least) as one grows older.

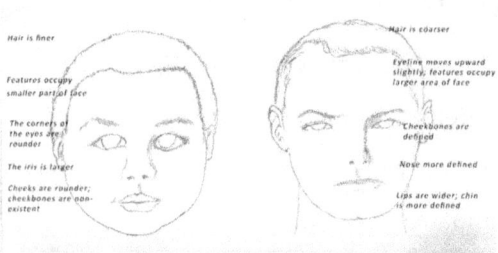

GENDER

The female face is often triangular, oval or heart-shaped, with soft edges. This contrasts with the sometimes (not always) square-jawed, sharp angular planes seen in men's faces. This is because the underlying skull and cranium are formed differently – full of sharp angles and planes in the male, whereas these bones are rounded with more curved edges in the female skull.

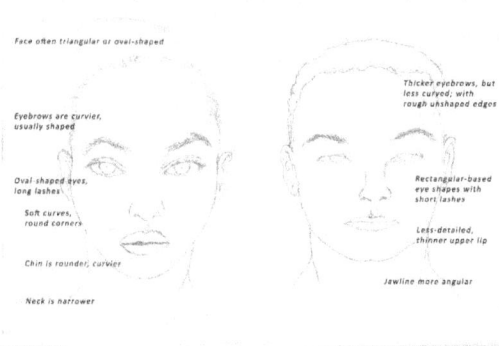

Face often triangular or oval-shaped

Eyebrows are curvier, usually shaped

Oval-shaped eyes, long lashes

Soft curves, round corners

Chin is rounder, curvier

Neck is narrower

Thicker eyebrows, but less curved; with rough unshaped edges

Rectangular-based eye shapes with short lashes

Less-detailed, thinner upper lip

Jawline more angular

The eyebrows in men are often fuller, thicker and 'unshaped', while those in women are thinner, and more curved. Conversely female eyelashes usually appear thicker (even without make-up), making the eyes appear larger with softer corners. Male eyelashes are sparser and the corners of the eyes are squarer (think of the more angular bony eye socket underneath).

The bridge of the nose is sharper and more chiseled in men. Their lips are wider and thinner; the jawline as we said earlier is more angular. Women's necks are thinner and slightly longer, while in the side-view the Adam's apple in men is more apparent. The hairline also recedes further back in men, and the forehead slopes more. In women the forehead is rounder and is almost always partly covered with hair. In men, the only facial hair we would expect to see is on the lower portion of the face.

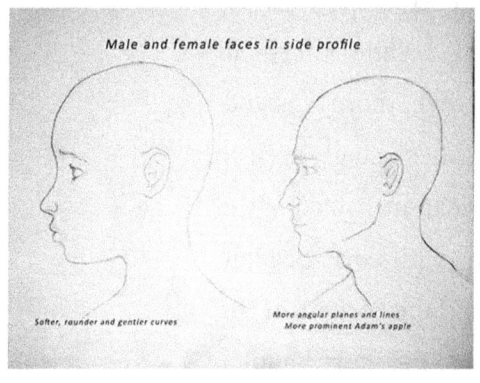

Male and female faces in side profile

Softer, rounder and gentler curves

More angular planes and lines
More prominent Adam's apple

These are only generalizations and principles to bear in mind, especially useful when rendering depicting generic human faces. Of course, individual differences would be more apparent as we zero in to the specific details of each portrait. These stereotypes merely serve as a 'know-the-rules-before-you-break-'em' guide.

RACE

There tend to be conflicts of opinion and disagreements regarding the major racial groups, especially because of lack of certainty regarding geographical origins. Nevertheless, we can consider the following major racial divisions:

1. Caucasoid (European)

2. Negroid (African)

3. Mongoloid (Asian)

4. Indic (Hindu)

5. Australian Aboriginal

6. American Indian

For the sake of simplicity, we shall examine the superficial differences among the first three main divisions.

Differences in stature: Caucasians are usually medium to tall, Mongoloids are mid-tall to mid-short, and Negroes cover a wider range, from tall to very short stature.

Facial (cranial) structure: this tends to be narrow to mid-broad in Caucasians and Negroes, and mid-broad to very broad in Mongoloids. There is also a tendency to strong prognathism in Negros, but none in Caucasians.

Hair: hair tends to be brown-black in Negroes, brownish to brown-black in Mongoloids, and a wider color range of light brown to dark brown in Caucasians. In the latter race, the form is also straight or wavy and the texture is fine, while it is straight with coarse texture in Mongoloids and woolly or frizzly with coarse texture in Negroes. Body hair is also sparse in Negroes and Mongoloids, and moderate or profuse in Caucasians.

Eyes: these are brown to brown-black in Negroes and Mongoloids, and a wider range of light blue to dark brown in Caucasians.

Nose structure: the nasal bridge is most often high and narrow to mid-broad in Caucasians, but low-placed and medium to very broad in Negros. In mongoloids the nasal features are in-between – low to medium-placed, and medium-broad in form.

Body shape: though you are hardly likely to venture below the chests of your portrait subjects, it is also good to keep in mind that the Negroid form is more often muscular while the Caucasian form is slenderer.

ACTION STEPS

Again, take a more detailed look at the photographs and faces of people close to you, or of pictures pulled from the internet. Look for the features we've described in their facial features. Now practice drawing some of these features yourselves, exaggerating the differences e.g. the wide, angular jawline in men; the shaped, curvier eyebrows in women.

Of course as we said earlier, the rules are made to be broken (in art, anyway). As we go into the more practical steps of the drawing process in the next chapters, please keep these distinctions at the back of your mind so they would assist you in passing across the authenticity of your subject.

CHAPTER 6. FREEHAND OR THE GRID?

NOW let's get down to real drawing!

But first, we need to sketch in the basic outlines of the face. If you have tried even unsuccessfully to draw a portrait true-to-life before, you would realize that a slight shift in the location or shape of the features could go a long way to affect the accuracy of your reproduction.

Hence we need to get these dimensions right from the start. To do this we have the options of either sketching in the features by freehand, or using a grid.

FREEHAND SKETCHING

This entails lightly marking the boundaries of the main features – eyebrows, eyes, nose, mouth and other particularly distinguishing features – on your paper. You would have gotten with a ruler the dimensions of the length and width of the face, width of the hairline, the distance of the eyebrows, from the eyes, nostrils and lips from the other boundaries of the face. Using the ruler, now translate these dimensions onto your paper lightly with an HB pencil.

You cannot do freehand sketching without having some important reference points. One of these is the width of the eye. You can use the width of one eye to estimate and 'mark off' other features such as the distances between both medial canthuses (the inner corners) of both eyes, the width of the nose and the lips, the distance between them both as well as from the lips to the chin.

Here are a few guides to keep in mind, generally common for most faces:

- *A line passing through the eyes would also mark the upper ends of both ears.*

- *The face at the level of the eyes is approximately five eyes wide. Note though that the distance between the two eyes is usually wider than the width of an eye.*

- *A line touching the outermost part of the nostril on each side would pass through the inner corners of both eyes.*

- *The ears in front view are about the length of the nose, from top to bottom.*

- *A line through the closed lips is usually halfway between the base of the nose and the chin.*

THE GRID METHOD

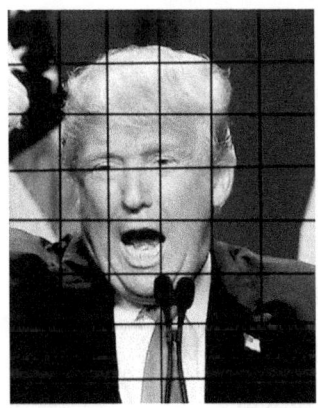

This is more precise and arguably more accurate, though more time-consuming. You are also likely to deface the photographs you are modelling from, something to keep in mind.

Essentially you would draw a 4-6 rows by 4 columns grid on the photograph, then draw the same number of guidelines very lightly on your paper very lightly with an HB or B pencil. I would not advise you use a hard (H to 6H) pencil to do this, as you could inadvertently indent the paper, which could later affect your shading.

Some people instead draw the gridlines with a black pen or very dark pencil on a sheet of paper which is then placed under the sheet of paper that will be drawn on. Also if the photograph is a digital one on your computer, you could create the gridlines with Photoshop or some other software on a copy of the photograph as shown in the example above, so as to leave the original untouched.

When you have completed the guidelines similarly to what you have on the photograph, you then carefully sketch in the shapes within the grid on the paper.

In my earlier days of portraiture, I used mainly the freehand method because I did not know any other way to keep from defacing the paper – as well as the photograph. As I taught myself, I automatically learnt to compare the width of the eye to the other features of the face. As I developed and learnt more, I began to combine both methods.

The important principle to note is that the original sketch is the make-or-break stage of your portrait. Take your time to establish boundaries, draw lines and place defining dots where lines and shapes intersect, so as to establish as exact a representation as possible. It does not matter how weird the features appear when you finish this stage, as long as you locate them aright. If you do not, your mistakes would be much more difficult to correct in later stages.

ACTION STEPS

Try using the grid method as well as the freehand sketching method for one of the photographs you feel most comfortable with. You do not need to be so accurate at this stage, just get used to both methods so as to familiarize yourself with them.

CHAPTER 7. WINDOWS TO THE SOUL

"The eyes are the windows to the soul". This statement holds particularly true with regard to portrait rendering. Ninety-five percent of times, you would find out that the expression of the subject is most clearly depicted by the eyes. Get them wrong, and the entire face would appear flat and lifeless.

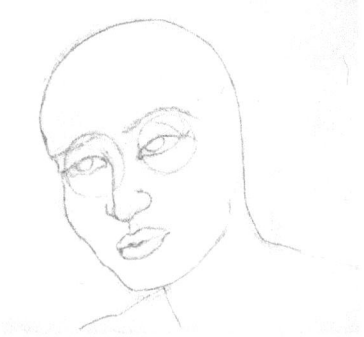

One good principle to remember is to always think in 3-D! The eyes are orbs inset within their sockets in the skull. The only parts that we actually see exposed by our eyelids is often less than one quarter of the entire surface area. However, you should always ensure you keep this spherical nature of the eyes in mind when drawing, and strive as much as possible to convey it to your viewers.

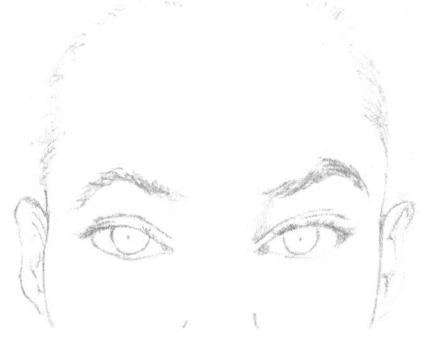

THE EYEBROWS...

...are placed above the orbs of the eyes, and follow the natural curvature of the forehead. Remember that they also help define the overall expression of the face.

The upper eyelashes curve away from the eyeballs; their bushiness varies with the subject. DO NOT draw them as evenly-placed strands.

Remember that both eyelids follow the curvature of the eyeball, i.e. think of the upper and lower eyelids as partly open spherical shells around the orb of the eye.

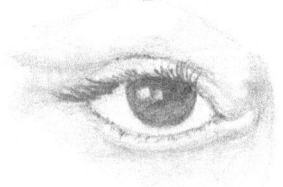

(Fun fact: the eyeballs are not purely spherical in shape, but are actually ellipsoidal – they would appear like slightly squashed eggs if you were looking at them from the sides.) Alright, let's get back to work!

The lower eyelashes are scantier, and are usually clumped together.

THE IRIS –

– watch out for this one. Not only is it usually the most interesting part of the eye to render, it is also the make-or-break stage of the eye.

Note that you hardly ever see the upper border of the iris – except when the eyes are very wide open as in surprise, shock, etc. In such cases the pupils are also slightly enlarged (dilated); otherwise they are mere black holes spot center of the irises – black holes which should nevertheless be drawn in unless they are obscured by highlights.

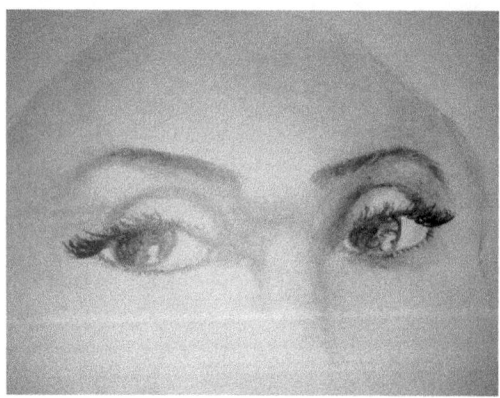

The degree to which the eyes are open or shut would also determine how much of the lower border of the iris is shown. In younger faces with wide open eyes, the lower border of the iris would lightly graze the lower eyelid, while in older people or squinting/half-open eyes, up to half the lower radius of the iris could be obscured by the lower eyelid and eyelashes. Think of the face as looking straight ahead, and the iris like the sun just rising above the horizon (which in this case is the lower eyelid).

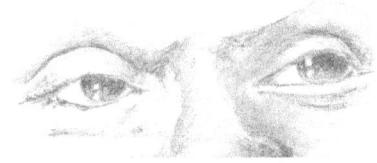

Remember also to show or at least hint at the radial pattern within the iris, especially in paler-colored eyes. This radial pattern is due to the two muscle groups within the iris which contract or relax together to widen or narrow the aperture of the pupil and allow light in to the inner chamber of the eyes. Almost exactly like a camera lens.

When shading the iris, keep the principles of shading a sphere in mind. Carefully place the highlights based on the direction of the primary light source similarly on both irises, as well as at least one or more secondary highlights as appropriate.

The highlights on the iris are the cream of the pudding, as it were. They are what give the eyes life and make them jump out at the viewers.

ACTION STEPS:

Get some picture references and sketch out and shade as many eyes as you can. Even if you cannot find any, get a mirror and draw your own eyes from different views, with different expressions. You would be amazed at the variety you can get even with your face alone. If you get digital photo references, zoom in and study the eyes up close. Enough practice with references and you would be able to draw well enough without any.

Chapter 8. The Nose Knows

Structurally the nose is the easiest feature to draw, and the least likely to affect the integrity of your drawing – as long as you do not render a big shapeless gunk of flesh. Remember it is centrally placed, so you either fill its shapes in subtly, allowing it to play a background role. Or you enlarge it and inadvertently cause it to draw attention from more important areas of the face.

Following our previous advice of 'thinking in 3-D' we can simplify the nose into a pyramid and two small spheres.

Noses come in all shapes and sizes, from the small roundish stubs we are usually born with...

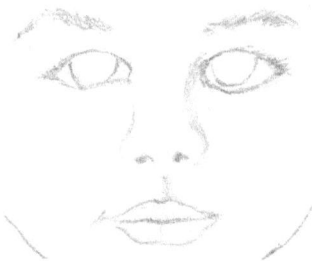

...To the more defined hooters we carry around as adults...

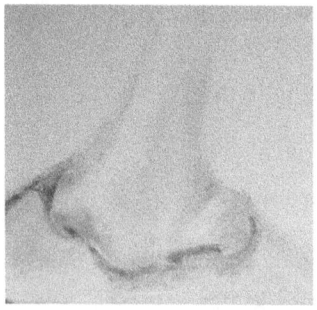

The nose may seem tricky to draw accurately, but by reducing it to the barest shapes as we would other areas, it can be done.

It is in rendering the nose that I will mention a principle which would also stand you in good stead in other areas of the face: eliminate the initial outlines and try to blend them and 'carve out' the nose from its adjoining shapes and structures. As much as possible, avoid leaving obvious outlines in your portrait drawing. They don't exist in real life, remember? The sketch below illustrates what I mean.

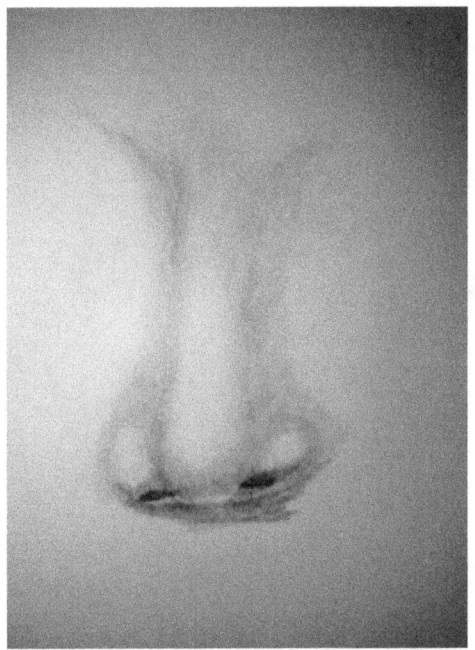

ACTION STEPS

Do several trial drawings of noses; yours as well as samples from various photographs. Like other features of the face you have practiced with, you would get a lot of variety from looking at your own nose from different angles in the mirror.

CHAPTER 9. CRAFTING THE LIPS

Next to the eyes, the lips are the most distinctive features of the face. Getting their shapes right is critical to establishing the exact expression and identity of your subjects.

The lips are all curvy shapes and smooth edges. You could see them as comprising a series of small spheres. So when shading them, use numerous gentle lines which follow the natural curvature of the lips.

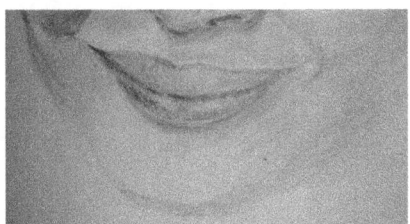

Remember the philtrum. Not that obvious in many subjects, but you should still leave a hint nevertheless.

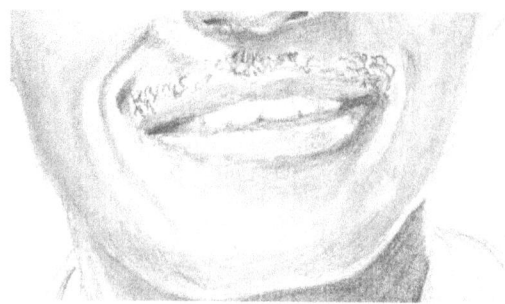

The 'bulb' of the upper lip slightly overhangs the lower one, so remember to put a line of shadow on the latter – unless the mouth is open.

In conclusion: the lips in conjunction with the eyes help convey a multitude of expressions. The more you practice drawing these features, the more accurately you would be able to communicate the true spirit of your subjects.

ACTION STEPS

Just like you did for the eyes, draw the lips in as many different expressions as you can – grinning, smiling, laughing, surprised, angry, etc. Let the mirror be your friend. Draw eyes and lips together in specific expressions, and your confidence would increase. Mastering facial expressions like this is necessary to be able to excel at cartooning and similar jobs.

Chapter 10. FROM EAR TO THERE

I smile as I write this because, for most artists who have not learnt to make sense of the seemingly confusing twists and turns of the outer ear, they just attach lumps of flesh to the sides of the face and try to avoid drawing the subject in a side view or three-quarter view.

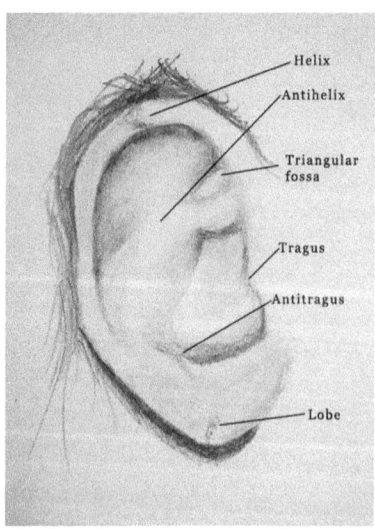

But as you can see, there is no cause for alarm. Once you get the major outlines down pat you will never forget them again.

Just like riding a bike, eh?

ACTION STEPS

Keep in mind the different anatomical landmarks of the ear as shown in the diagram above. That way, when you draw different variations of the ear as it appears in different subjects, you would not miss out the major anatomical landmarks.

Chapter 11. Hair Job

Another scary and probably tricky stage for the uninitiated, but once you begin to get the hang of it, you can even begin to flaunt your skills!

Remember our recurring theme, "Think in 3D"? Look at the hair as made up of several shapes – bands and masses – which you need to depict as such, and not just as individual strands of hair.

When shading the hair, no matter its color you should be able to establish at least three values – mid-tones, darks and highlights. This would help nail the authenticity of your reproduction.

First, start with a general sketch outlining your subject's hair:

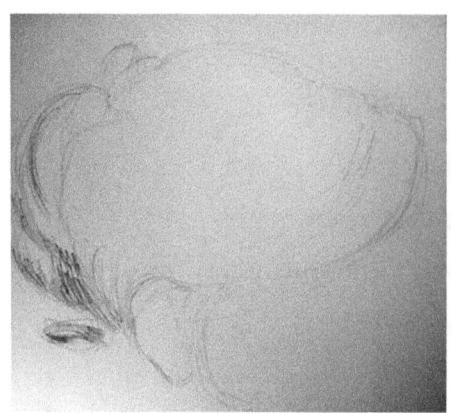

Then put in mid-tones, taking care not to block in the areas you would place your highlights. Take your time to build up the hair over several layers:

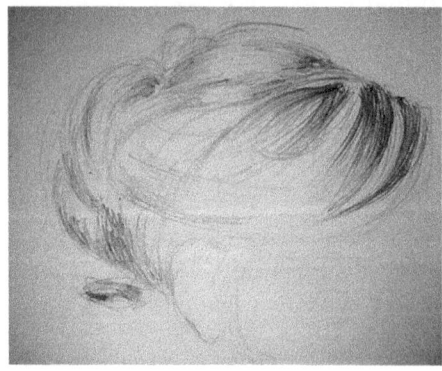

Then fill in your darks...

... And lastly come the highlights, which must be in line with the predominant light source.

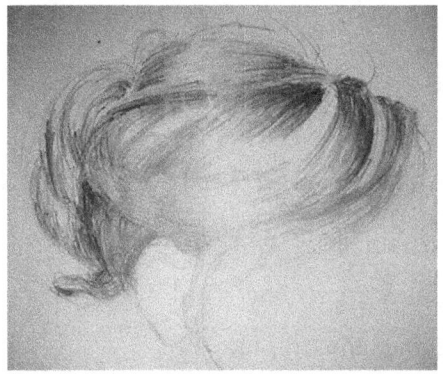

ACTION STEPS:

Now we have gone through all the main landmarks and features of the face. You should be courageous enough to try out some complete faces of your own. If you haven't already, dust off that old photo album, pull out your sketchbook and get cracking once again!

Chapter 12. PROTECT YOUR WORK

Whether you are going to frame your portrait immediately or not, it would be wise to take steps to prevent smudging.

Even if you place your finished work between two sheets of paper, or frame it immediately, chances are that the graphite could get smeared unto the protective sheet of paper or unto the glass sheet of your frame, if it comes into contact with it. This is one instance where the same qualities that makes pencils a joy to work with, make it a pain to preserve.

For such situations, a Fixative spray would come in handy. It would be worthwhile to invest in a quality product right from the start. Thus you would be sure of your paper not changing color any time soon.

Remember to apply any finishing touches and sign your work as well, before applying the fixative. Once you spray your work you would not be able to erase it because it would be covered by a thin layer of varnish. You could still draw upon this, but it could never be the same as the pure paper surface.

CHAPTER 13. A TRIAL
EXAMPLE

In this example, we'll run through the steps it takes to create a speed-draw portrait from the photograph below:

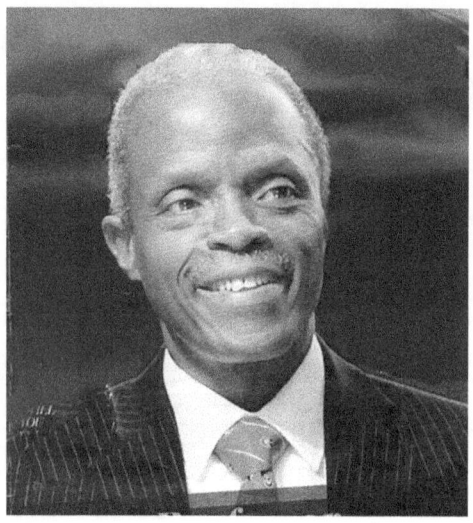

In this example we utilize the freehand method to outline our initial sketch:

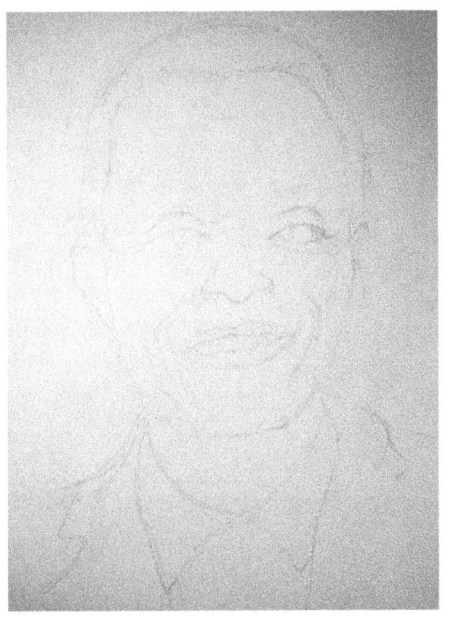

Then we begin to fill in the shapes with different shading styles as we learnt earlier, working from the upper left, down to the lower right so as to avoid smudging...

(Of course, if you are left-handed you would begin from the upper right corner and fill in your drawing to the lower right.) The point to keep in mind is to avoid placing any of your hands on your work as much as possible. And if you absolutely have to, you should place a piece of white paper or cardboard underneath to protect your work.

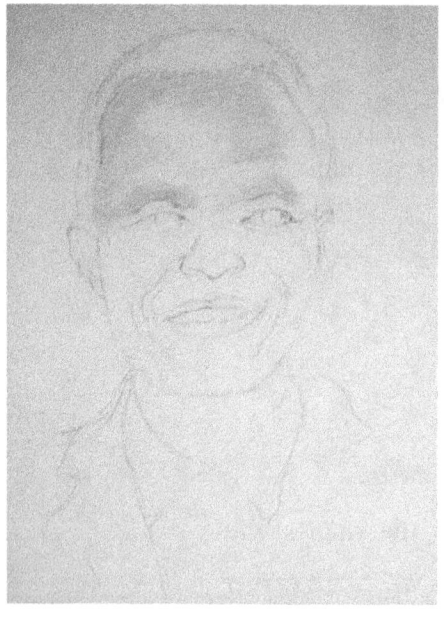

Slowly and patiently we shade in the features. You need to develop the light and dark areas in several passes – when shading a particularly dark area, shade gently and blend two or more times so it would be easier to retrace your steps if necessary...

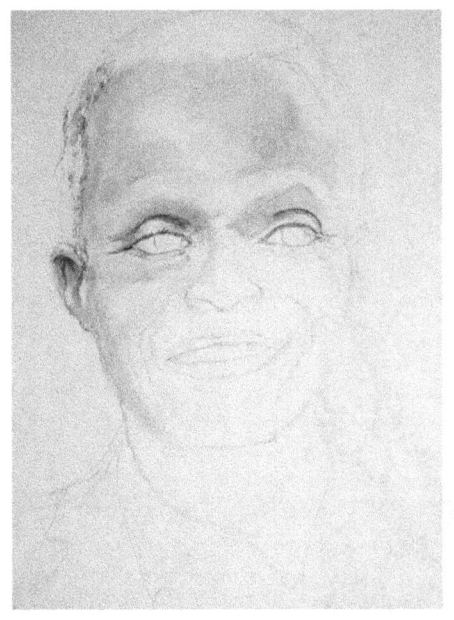

When to complete the eyes? Different portraiture artists have different ideas about this. Some prefer to fill in the eyes as they cover that particular area of the face, so they would not have to go back to it. Others prefer to leave the eyes blank until every other feature is completed and refined, and then bring the whole face to life by filling in the eyes as the 'final touch', so to speak.

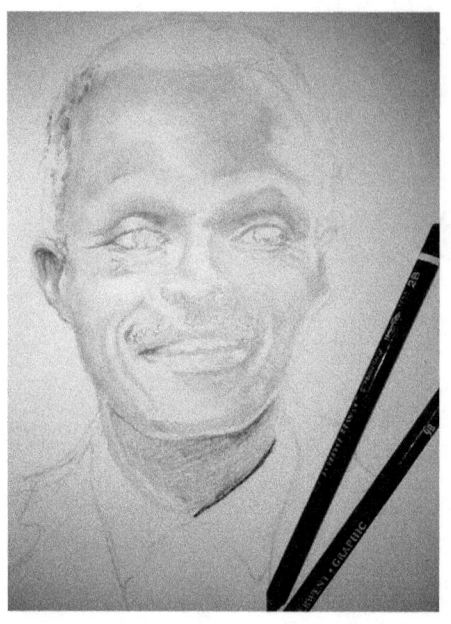

Personally I prefer something in-between, though leaning toward the latter – I do not wait for the entire face to be completed before I draw in the eyes, but as soon as the drawing has reached such a stage that some critical areas have been finalized, then I shade the eyes. Whichever method you adopt, take your time with them.

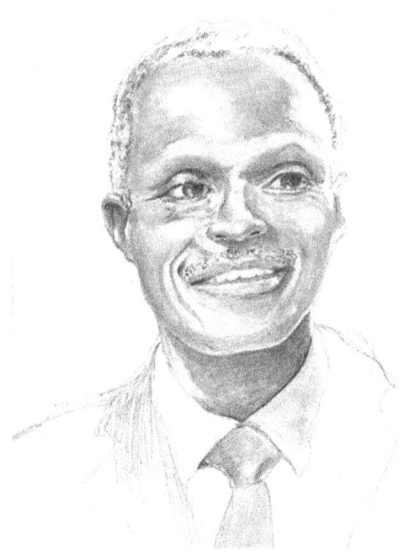

And...*voila!* It would be necessary to fill in the pattern of the jacket as well as a few other details, but everything else from here would be a piece of cake, wouldn't it?

ONE LAST THING...

If you enjoyed this book or found it useful I'd be very grateful if you'd post a short review on Amazon. Your support really does make a difference and I read all the reviews personally so I can get your feedback and make this book even better.

Thanks again for your support!

www.ingramcontent.com/pod-product-compliance
Lightning Source LLC
Chambersburg PA
CBHW051816170526
45167CB00005B/2043